Introduction:

Welcome to the fascinating universe of Ethereum, a revolutionary ecosystem propelling far beyond the borders of digital finance. Imagine a space where transactions are no longer just monetary exchanges but self-executing contracts, where applications can function without central authority, and where innovation fuels every line of code.

This book serves as your ticket to explore the depths of this blockchain platform. Ethereum, more than just a cryptocurrency, embodies a technological revolution. It's a blank canvas for creative minds, a decentralized infrastructure redefining how we conceptualize trust, write contracts, and build applications.

Within these pages, you'll discover how Ethereum evolved from a bold vision to a revolutionary reality. We delve into its foundations, exploring the magic of smart contracts, unraveling the intricate mechanisms of the blockchain, and navigating a dynamic ecosystem of innovative projects.

But Ethereum is much more than a technology; it's a global community of innovators, developers, and thinkers shaping the future of finance, governance, and beyond. We explore the ethical issues, regulatory challenges, and promises of empowerment that this revolution brings.

Through these pages, we delve into the depths of a constantly evolving technology, examining its impact on the global economy, its potential to shape our societies, and its role in transforming numerous sectors.

This book is a journey through the depths of the blockchain, where each chapter is an open window into a constantly changing world, where innovation and collaboration sketch a promising future.

Join us in exploring Ethereum, from its roots to its branches, from its challenges to its triumphs, and discover how this technological revolution defines our tomorrow.

Contents

Introduction:

1. Presentation of Ethereum as a programmable blockchain platform.
2. The history of Ethereum: its genesis.

Chapter 1: Foundations of Ethereum

1. Explanation of the concept of smart contracts and the Ethereum Virtual Machine (EVM).
2. Basic architecture of Ethereum: blockchain, blocks, and transactions.

Chapter 2: The Ethereum Ecosystem

1. Exploration of major cryptocurrencies based on Ethereum (ERC-20 tokens).
2. In-depth case studies of notable applications and projects on Ethereum.

Chapter 3: Smart Contracts and Development on Ethereum

1. In-depth understanding of smart contracts: functioning and utilities.
2. Practical guide to developing smart contracts on the Ethereum platform.

Chapter 4: Proof of Stake (PoS)

1. Explanation of the transition from Proof-of-Work (PoW) to Proof-of-Stake (PoS).
2. Environmental benefits and security associated with PoS.

Chapter 5: Scalability and Ethereum 2.0

1. Ethereum's scalability challenges and proposed solutions.
2. Introduction of Ethereum 2.0, the concept of sharding, and technical updates.

Chapter 6: Projects and Decentralized Applications (DApps)

1. Exploration of popular DApps on the Ethereum blockchain.
2. Ethereum's impact on the development of decentralized applications.

Chapter 7: DeFi (Decentralized Finance) on Ethereum

1. Introduction to major DeFi protocols built on Ethereum.
2. Analysis of opportunities and challenges in the DeFi sector.

Chapter 8: Regulatory and Legal Evolution of Ethereum

1. Current state of regulations related to Ethereum on a global scale.
2. Implications of regulatory developments on Ethereum adoption.

Chapter 9: The Ethereum Community

Role of the community in the continuous development of Ethereum.

Chapter 10: Ethereum and Technological Innovation

1. Latest technological developments on Ethereum.
2. Potential impacts on the future of blockchain and decentralized applications.

Chapter 11: Economic Analysis and Price Evolution

Exploration of Ethereum's economic impact and factors influencing ETH price.

Chapter 12: Ethical and Social Issues

Reflection on the ethical implications of using Ethereum and its social impact.

Chapter 13: Trends and Future Predictions

Exploration of future forecasts and trends for Ethereum, including possible scenarios.

Chapter 14: Security and Vulnerabilities of Ethereum

1. In-depth analysis of past security flaws on Ethereum.
2. Presentation of current security measures and security trends on the platform.

Chapter 15: Advanced Technical Evolution

1. Exploration of ongoing research and advanced technical developments on Ethereum.
2. Perspectives on possible evolutions of protocols and technologies associated with Ethereum.

Chapter 16: Ethereum Economy and Ecosystem

1. Study of Ethereum's internal economy, including transaction pricing models, incentives for miners and validators, etc.
2. Analysis of Ethereum's impact on the global cryptocurrency economy.

Chapter 17: Adoption, Usage, and Real-World Use Cases

1. Study of real-world use cases of Ethereum in different sectors (finance, supply chain, governance, etc.).
2. Evaluation of Ethereum's adoption by businesses and end-users.

Chapter 18: Education, Training, and Resources

1. Resources for learning and training on Ethereum: guides, tutorials, and best practices.
2. Education and awareness initiatives for Ethereum worldwide.

Chapter 19: Summary of External

Perspectives Interviews or contributions from external experts offering diverse perspectives on the future of Ethereum and blockchain technology.

Chapter 20: Global and Geopolitical

Perspectives Analysis of Ethereum's impact and adoption in different geographical and socio-economic contexts worldwide.

Chapter 21: Partnerships and Collaboration

1. Collaboration with other renowned blockchains and protocols.
2. Impact of partnerships on the Ethereum ecosystem and blockchain in general.

Chapter 22: Advanced Concepts and Technical Developments

1. In-depth exploration of emerging concepts such as rollups, secondary scaling solutions.
2. Advances in privacy and security: zero-knowledge proofs, privacy techniques.

Chapter 23: Retrospective of Ethereum Versions

1. Detailed history of previous versions of Ethereum, highlighting the evolution of features and major updates.
2. Impacts of updates on the community and adoption of Ethereum.

Chapter 24: Deep Social and Ethical Impact

1. In-depth reflections on the positive social impact and ethical challenges related to the use of Ethereum in different socio-economic contexts.
2. Ethereum's potential for empowerment and reduction of inequalities in certain regions or industries

Chapter 25: International Adoption and Geopolitics

1. In-depth analysis of Ethereum adoption in various countries and regions, highlighting obstacles, opportunities, and cultural differences.
2. Geopolitical impact of the growing adoption of the Ethereum blockchain.

Chapter 26: Responses to Advanced Questions

1. Exploration of complex issues regarding Ethereum's governance, scalability, and other technical challenges.
2. Perspectives on potential solutions to these advanced questions.

Chapter 27: Current Developments and Projects to Watch

1. Highlights ongoing projects, upcoming updates, and emerging trends within the Ethereum ecosystem.
2. Potential impact of these developments on the future of Ethereum and blockchain technology.

Conclusion: Summary of Key Points.

Introduction:

1. Introduction to Ethereum as a programmable blockchain platform.

Ethereum, often described as the next revolutionary wave after Bitcoin, transcends simple notions of cryptocurrencies to offer much more: a programmable blockchain platform. Designed by the visionary Vitalik Buterin and his collaborators, this blockchain goes beyond mere value transactions to enable the execution of smart contracts.

At its core, Ethereum provides a decentralized infrastructure where users can build decentralized applications (DApps) and smart contracts. These smart contracts, at the heart of this innovation, are autonomous pieces of code that execute automatically when specific conditions are met. They can manage transactions, agreements, or even automate complex processes without the need for intermediaries.

This concept of the "Ethereum Virtual Machine" (EVM) is the backbone of this platform. The EVM is a secure and isolated execution environment where smart contracts are deployed and executed. This opens the door to a multitude of potential applications in various fields, from finance to logistics, governance, and beyond.

This book will delve into the depths of this revolutionary platform, exploring its foundations, its operation, and its impact on how we conceive and interact with technology. We closely examine how Ethereum has become more than just a blockchain but a dynamic canvas where innovation and creativity redefine the boundaries of what blockchain technology can achieve.

Join us in this captivating exploration of Ethereum's programmable universe, where every line of code written paves the way for new opportunities, shapes industries, and expands the horizons of technology.

2. The History of Ethereum: Its Genesis

Welcome to the ever-evolving universe of Ethereum, a technological revolution that transcends mere digital transactions. Ethereum is more than just a cryptocurrency; it's a programmable blockchain platform that redefines how we conceptualize and use technology.

Introducing Ethereum: A Revolutionary Vision

Ethereum isn't just a digital currency; it's fertile ground for innovation. It all began with Vitalik Buterin's enlightened vision in 2013 as he sought to push the boundaries of blockchain technology. His aim? To create a blockchain more dynamic than Bitcoin, a platform capable of much more than financial transactions. Thus, the concept of Ethereum was born—a programmable blockchain offering the ability to create smart contracts. Vitalik shared this revolutionary vision in the Ethereum Yellow Paper in 2014, laying the groundwork for what would become a platform propelling innovation worldwide.

The History of Ethereum: Its Genesis

In 2015, Ethereum transitioned from an idea to reality with the launch of its first version, Frontier. It was a pivotal moment, enabling developers to write smart contracts and build decentralized applications (DApps). This step opened the doors to an era of blockchain programmability, where every line of code was an opportunity to push the boundaries of technology. The beginnings were not without challenges: in 2016, the hacking of The DAO sparked profound discussions within the Ethereum community, highlighting governance issues in an evolving ecosystem.

This introduction marks the beginning of an in-depth exploration of Ethereum. We delve into its history, advanced techniques, societal impact, and examine how this platform has evolved to become more than just a blockchain but an agent of change in the world of technology.

Chapter 1: Foundations of Ethereum

1. Explanation of Smart Contracts and the Ethereum Virtual Machine (EVM).

Smart Contracts: Programmable Revolution

Smart contracts are the lifeblood of Ethereum, offering much more than simple transactions. Think of them as self-executing digital agreements. They are autonomous pieces of computer code stored on the blockchain and capable of automatically executing actions when they meet certain predefined conditions. These contracts enable process automation without the need for intermediaries. Their potential is vast, ranging from managing transactions to establishing complex agreements in various domains such as finance, governance, and much more.

The Ethereum Virtual Machine (EVM): The Engine of Innovation

The Ethereum Virtual Machine (EVM) is the engine behind the execution of smart contracts. It provides a secure execution environment where these contracts can be deployed and executed. Every node in the Ethereum network has a copy of the EVM, ensuring consistency and reliability in contract execution.

The EVM also enables interoperability of smart contracts, meaning they can interact with each other, paving the way for endless application scenarios.

Impact of Smart Contracts and the EVM

Smart contracts and the EVM have opened new vistas in terms of blockchain programmability. They have revolutionized how we conceptualize transactions, agreements, and decentralized applications. This advancement has spurred innovation by empowering developers to create customized, secure, and transparent solutions, thereby transforming how businesses, governments, and even individuals interact and conduct business.

2. Basic Architecture of Ethereum: Blockchain, Blocks, and Transactions.

The Blockchain: Pillar of Trust Ethereum's blockchain is a decentralized and secure data structure that records all transactions made on the network. It acts as a public ledger accessible to all network participants. Each block on the blockchain contains a set of verified transactions and is cryptographically linked to its predecessor, thus creating an immutable chain of blocks. This transparency and immutability form the foundation of trust within the Ethereum ecosystem.

Blocks: Links in the Chain Each block contains data about recent transactions and a cryptographic reference to the previous block. Miners, the entities responsible for securing and validating transactions, group these transactions into blocks, verify them, and then add them to the blockchain. This interconnected block structure ensures the continuity, security, and integrity of the Ethereum blockchain.

Transactions: Exchange of Value and Information Transactions on Ethereum represent the exchange of value or information between network users. They include operations such as cryptocurrency transfers (like ETH) or the execution of smart contracts. Each transaction is cryptographically signed to ensure its authenticity and security. Once validated by miners, these transactions become irreversible and are recorded on the blockchain for complete transparency.

The Essence of the Technology This foundational architecture shapes Ethereum's infrastructure, creating a transparent, secure, and decentralized ecosystem. The blockchain, with its blocks and transactions, is more than a mere infrastructure technique; it embodies the principles of trust, immutability, and freedom that fuel the revolutionary potential of this platform.

Chapter 2: The Ethereum Ecosystem

1. Exploration of Major Cryptocurrencies Based on Ethereum (ERC-20 Tokens).

ERC-20 Tokens: Foundations of Diversity

ERC-20 tokens are digital assets built on the Ethereum blockchain following a specific standard called ERC-20 (Ethereum Request for Comment 20). These tokens pioneered diversity within the Ethereum ecosystem, enabling the creation and exchange of a multitude of digital assets, such as tokens representing currencies, goods, stocks, or rights.

Characteristics of ERC-20 Tokens

ERC-20 tokens share common features: they can be easily traded, their issuance is controlled by smart contracts, and they follow a standardized set of rules, facilitating their use and interoperability across various platforms. These tokens have become an essential instrument for creating ICOs (Initial Coin Offerings) and numerous decentralized applications (DApps).

Diversity and Use of ERC-20 Tokens

The diversity of ERC-20 tokens is impressive. Some tokens represent innovative projects, emerging companies, or community initiatives, while others offer decentralized financial solutions or serve as utility tokens for specific platforms. These tokens are traded on trading platforms, used as means of payment or access to services, or held as investments.

Impact on the Ecosystem

ERC-20 tokens have played a significant role in expanding and diversifying the Ethereum ecosystem. They have enabled thousands of projects to leverage funds, innovate, and offer new forms of currency and utility in a decentralized ecosystem. However, their proliferation has also raised questions about regulation, security, and efficiency, posing challenges but also offering new opportunities.

2. In-depth Case Studies on Notable Applications and Projects on Ethereum.

Uniswap: Revolutionizing Decentralized Exchange (DEX)

Uniswap, a decentralized exchange platform (DEX), stands as a prime example of the power of DApps on Ethereum. Using smart contracts, Uniswap enables anyone to exchange ERC-20 tokens without intermediaries. Its automated liquidity provision model has opened new exchange opportunities, fostering innovation in the realm of decentralized exchanges.

MakerDAO and Dai: Stability Amid Volatility

MakerDAO introduced Dai, a stablecoin (a cryptocurrency pegged to a stable asset like the US dollar) operating on Ethereum. Dai offers stability in an ecosystem often characterized by diversity. Using intricate mechanisms harnessed through smart contracts, MakerDAO created a decentralized stablecoin solution, providing a unique alternative in the world of cryptocurrencies.

Axie Infinity: Blockchain Game and NFT Economy

Axie Infinity is an Ethereum blockchain-based game that has captivated thousands of players with its innovative economic model. Axie Infinity employs non-fungible tokens (NFTs) to represent unique in-game creatures. Players can own, breed, and trade these creatures, creating a thriving virtual economy around the game.

Gitcoin: Funding Open Source Projects

Gitcoin is a platform that connects developers with open-source projects, allowing them to receive funding through mechanisms managed by smart contracts. By utilizing the Ethereum blockchain, Gitcoin fosters growth and innovation in the world of open-source software development.

Impact of Case Studies

These case studies offer insights into the endless possibilities offered by Ethereum. They illustrate how blockchain technology can be used to reinvent financial exchanges, create new economic models, revolutionize online gaming, and even support the development of open-source software. These notable projects serve as tangible examples of the impact and diversity within the Ethereum ecosystem.

Chapter 3: Smart Contracts and Development on Ethereum

1. **In-depth Understanding of Smart Contracts: Functionality and Uses.**

Functioning of Smart Contracts

Smart contracts are self-executing programs hosted on the Ethereum blockchain. They are written in programming languages like Solidity and operate as digital contracts, executing predefined actions when specific conditions are met. Once deployed on the blockchain, these contracts run automatically and immutably, without the possibility of manipulation.

Uses of Smart Contracts

The uses of smart contracts are extensive and diverse. They are used to create automated payment systems, execute digital agreements, facilitate financial transactions, and much more. Their utility also extends to decentralized applications (DApps), where they serve as the foundation for transparently executing specific functions without requiring intermediaries.

Advantages and Challenges

The advantages of smart contracts lie in their immutability, transparency, and automation. However, they are not without challenges. Programming complexity, security issues, and code errors can lead to unforeseen consequences. Past incidents, such as The DAO hack, highlighted the need for rigorous audits and good development practices to ensure the reliability of smart contracts.

Impact on the Ecosystem

Smart contracts are the pillar upon which much of the innovation on Ethereum rests. They have paved the way for a new era of digital trust, enabling secure and automated transactions without requiring levels of trust. Their transformative potential continues to catalyze the development of new business models, reinvent financial systems, and foster the emergence of decentralized solutions.

2. Practical Guide to Developing Smart Contracts on the Ethereum Platform.

Initial Steps

Understanding the Basics: Before diving in, familiarize yourself with Solidity, the most commonly used programming language for smart contracts on Ethereum. Resources like Ethereum's official documentation, online tutorials, and developer communities can be helpful.

Development Environment: Set up your development environment. Tools like Remix, Truffle, or Hardhat provide testing and deployment environments for writing, testing, and deploying smart contracts.

Development Process

Design and Planning: Understand the requirements and logic of your smart contract. Define its functionalities, conditions, and interactions with other contracts or users.

Writing Code: Begin writing your smart contract in Solidity. Follow best coding practices to ensure code security and reliability.

Testing and Debugging: Test your smart contract on a test network (like Rinkeby or Ropsten) to verify its functionality. Conduct thorough tests to detect and fix errors.

Deployment: Once your smart contract is tested and functioning correctly, deploy it on the Ethereum network. Ensure you understand the gas costs associated with deployment.

Best Practices and Security

Audit and Security: Consider getting your smart contract audited by third parties to identify potential vulnerabilities.

Key and Permission Management: Secure the private keys used to deploy or interact with contracts. Use appropriate access modifiers to manage permissions.

Evolution and Maintenance

Updates: Plan for update mechanisms if necessary. Understand the impact of changes on deployed contracts and their compatibility with previous versions.

Documentation: Thoroughly document your code to facilitate future understanding and maintenance.

Community and Resources

Engage with the Ethereum developer community, participate in forums, discussion groups, and hackathons to stay updated with the latest advancements and benefit from other developers' experiences.

Chapter 4: Proof of Stake (PoS) Consensus

1. **Explanation of the Transition from Proof-of-Work (PoW) to Proof-of-Stake (PoS).**

Proof-of-Work (PoW): Foundation of Security

Proof-of-Work is the original consensus mechanism used by Ethereum (and also by Bitcoin). In this system, miners solve complex mathematical problems to validate transactions and create new blocks. This method relies on significant computational power and consumes a significant amount of energy.

Transition to Proof-of-Stake (PoS): A Paradigm Shift

The transition from PoW to PoS is a major evolution for Ethereum. Proof-of-Stake replaces the computational power competition with a logic of ownership and validation based on staking assets. Rather than requiring miners, PoS relies on validators who are chosen to validate transactions based on the amount of ETH they stake as collateral.

Advantages of Proof-of-Stake

Energy Efficiency: PoS is considerably more energy-efficient compared to PoW since it doesn't require intensive calculations.

Security: Participants risk their assets, which is expected to deter them from engaging in malicious behavior.

Democratization: PoS makes consensus participation more accessible to a larger number of people due to the potential centralization induced by large miners.

Ethereum 2.0 and the Transition:

The transition from PoW to PoS is a key element of Ethereum 2.0, the next major iteration of the Ethereum network. This ambitious upgrade aims to enhance the network's scalability, security, and efficiency. The transition phase to PoS began with the launch of the Beacon Chain in December 2020, marking the start of a PoS era for Ethereum.

Challenges and Issues:

Although PoS offers many advantages, there are challenges to overcome, including security and resilience to attacks. Researchers and developers are working on these issues to ensure the robustness of the new consensus model.

2. Environmental Advantages and Security Associated with PoS

Enhanced Security of PoS

Energy Efficiency: PoS is considered more environmentally friendly than PoW because it doesn't require intensive computational power. Unlike PoW, which uses massive amounts of electricity to power miners, PoS operates with a considerably reduced energy footprint.

Carbon Footprint Reduction: By eliminating the need for extensive mining farms, PoS contributes to reducing the carbon footprint associated with validating transactions and creating new blocks on the blockchain.

Improved Security of PoS

Stake and Security: In PoS, validators (who stake and manage cryptocurrency holdings) secure the network by staking their assets. The risk of losing their funds incentivizes validators to play an honest and secure role, creating a security incentive mechanism.

Reduction in 51% Attacks: Unlike PoW, where an entity holding more than 50% of the computational power could manipulate the network, PoS would make such attacks costly and impractical. Owning the majority of assets would require a disproportionate amount of cryptocurrency, making it unprofitable for an attack.

Evolution of Security:

While PoS offers several advantages in terms of security and energy efficiency, it's essential to note that each consensus model has its own challenges and vulnerabilities. Researchers and developers continue to work on enhancing the resilience of PoS and mitigating any potential risks associated with this new mechanism.

Chapter 5: Scalability and Ethereum 2.0

1. Scalability Challenges of Ethereum and Proposed Solutions

Scalability Challenges

High Network Traffic: The Ethereum network faces increasing congestion due to the rise of decentralized applications (DApps), causing delays in transaction confirmations and high gas fees. •

Transaction Limit: Ethereum, in its current state, can process only a limited number of transactions per second, becoming a bottleneck as the demand for fast and cheap transactions grows.

Proposed Solutions

Ethereum 2.0: This major upgrade aims to address scalability issues. It introduces the shift from PoW to PoS, sharding implementation, and consensus mechanism optimization to enhance network performance.

Sharding: Ethereum 2.0 proposes sharding, dividing the blockchain into smaller sections called "shards." Each shard can process its set of transactions, distributing the load across multiple parallel chains and increasing the network's capacity.

Technical Updates: Improvements like introducing rollups (layer two scaling technologies) and other layer two solutions are also considered to increase transaction processing capacity without compromising network security.

Changes for the Ecosystem

Enhanced User Experience: Scalability solutions envisioned for Ethereum 2.0 aim to provide an improved user experience with faster transactions, reduced gas costs, and greater DApp utilization capacity.

Diversification of Use Cases: By boosting network capacity, Ethereum 2.0 paves the way for new use cases, including applications requiring large-scale transactions like payments, online gaming, and complex decentralized systems.

Ongoing Evolution

Scalability remains an ongoing challenge for Ethereum. While Ethereum 2.0 proposes ambitious solutions, technological development is an iterative process, and continuous adjustments and improvements will be necessary to maintain the network's competitiveness and efficiency.

2. Introduction to Ethereum 2.0, Sharding Concept, and Technical Updates

Ethereum 2.0: An Ambitious Upgrade

Transition from PoW to PoS: Ethereum 2.0 signifies a major transformation of the consensus protocol, shifting from Proof-of-Work (PoW) to Proof of Stake (PoS). This evolution aims to enhance energy efficiency, security, and the scalability of the Ethereum network.

Deployment Phases: Ethereum 2.0 deployment is divided into phases. The initial phase commenced with the Beacon Chain, introducing PoS and paving the way for a PoS network. Future phases include the introduction of sharding and other enhancements.

Sharding Concept: Horizontal Expansion of the Blockchain

Division into Shards: Sharding divides the Ethereum blockchain into smaller sections called "shards." Each shard operates independently, processing its set of transactions. This approach allows Ethereum to achieve horizontal expansion, significantly increasing its overall processing capacity.

Enhancing Scalability: By distributing transactions among shards, the sharding concept aims to substantially boost the network throughput, enabling Ethereum to process a more extensive number of transactions simultaneously.

Technical Updates of Ethereum 2.0

Rollups and Other Layer 2 Solutions: Ethereum 2.0 contemplates the integration of rollups, secondary scaling solutions that aggregate numerous off-chain transactions onto the main blockchain, thus alleviating the load on the main network.

Protocol Optimizations: Developers are working on technical improvements to make the network more efficient, secure, and user-friendly, including enhancing transaction confirmation times and, notably, gas fees.

Impact of Ethereum 2.0

Improved Scalability: Ethereum 2.0 aims to address the network's scalability challenges, providing an infrastructure capable of supporting massive transaction fees while maintaining reasonable costs and rapid confirmation times.

Exploration of New Use Cases: By offering better scalability, Ethereum 2.0 could foster the emergence of new applications and use cases requiring fast and cost-effective transactions.

Conclusion Ethereum 2.0 represents a significant evolution in the blockchain world, striving to make Ethereum more scalable, secure, and efficient. While the transition is gradual, the improvements brought by Ethereum 2.0 have the potential to transform how decentralized applications are developed and utilized.

Chapter 6: Decentralized Applications (DApps)

1. Exploration of Popular DApps on the Ethereum Blockchain

DeFi (Decentralized Finance)

Uniswap: A decentralized exchange platform (DEX) enabling intermediary-free transactions.

Aave: A lending and borrowing protocol offering the opportunity to earn interest on deposited cryptocurrencies.

Games and Entertainment

Decentraland: A virtual world where users can buy, sell, and develop virtual real estate.

Axie Infinity: A game involving the collection and breeding of digital creatures, allowing players to earn and trade tokens.

NFTs (Non-Fungible Tokens)

CryptoPunks: A collection of 10,000 unique punks, a pioneer in the NFT space.

OpenSea: A marketplace platform for trading NFTs, offering a variety of digital artwork, virtual lands, etc.

Governance and Decentralized Organizations

MakerDAO: A lending protocol and stablecoin managed by a decentralized autonomous organization (DAO).

DAOstack: A governance platform enabling the creation and management of custom DAOs.

Impact of DApps

Growing Adoption: Ethereum-based DApps are gaining popularity due to their decentralized nature, offering increased transparency and user autonomy. Challenges Ahead: Despite their growth, DApps face challenges such as user experience, scalability, and high gas fees.

Continued Innovation: Ethereum's DApps represent a fraction of the potential use cases for blockchain technology. Innovation continues with new projects aiming to solve existing problems and explore new application domains.

Global Accessibility: Ethereum has democratized the development of decentralized applications, enabling individuals and small businesses worldwide to create DApps without the approval of third parties or centralized entities.

Smart Contracts: Smart contracts have revolutionized application programming by eliminating the need for intermediaries. They enable the automatic execution of autonomous contracts without requiring mutual trust.

Emergence of New Economic Models

Decentralized Finance (DeFi): Ethereum has propelled DeFi by creating lending, exchange, and fund management protocols without traditional banking infrastructure.

Non-Fungible Tokens (NFTs): The issuance of non-fungible tokens on Ethereum has enabled new economic models for artists and creators, allowing authenticated digital ownership and monetization of digital works.

Decentralization of Governance

Decentralized Autonomous Organizations (DAOs): Ethereum has facilitated the emergence of DAOs, enabling users to participate in project governance transparently and democratically.

Open Governance: Users directly influence protocol development and updates, shifting control from the hands of a few to the distributed community.

Continuous Technological Evolution

Interoperability: Ethereum has spurred innovation in interoperability, allowing different blockchains to work together, with projects such as Polkadot and Cosmos.

Transition to Ethereum 2.0: The transition to Ethereum 2.0 signifies continued commitment to improving scalability, security, and network efficiency, potentially significantly impacting DApp development and usage.

Conclusion

Ethereum's impact on the development of decentralized applications has been monumental, ushering in a new era of innovation in the blockchain world. With ever-evolving technology, the Ethereum ecosystem remains at the heart of the decentralized revolution.

2. Impact of Ethereum on the Development of Decentralized Applications

Democratization of Development

Global Access: Ethereum has opened doors for developers worldwide to create decentralized applications without requiring approval from third parties or centralized entities. This has enabled individuals and small businesses to actively participate in blockchain development.

Smart Contracts: Smart contracts on Ethereum have revolutionized how applications are programmed. By eliminating the need for intermediaries, Ethereum has made it possible to create autonomous contracts that execute automatically without the need for mutual trust.

Emergence of New Economic Models

Decentralized Finance (DeFi): Ethereum has catalyzed the development of DeFi by creating lending, exchange, and fund management protocols without the need for traditional banking infrastructure. Users can engage in decentralized financial services directly from their Ethereum wallets.

Non-Fungible Tokens (NFTs): The issuance of non-fungible tokens on Ethereum has given rise to new economic models for artists, content creators, and virtual asset owners. NFTs allow authenticated digital ownership and monetization of digital works.

Decentralization of Governance

Decentralized Autonomous Organizations (DAOs): Ethereum has facilitated the emergence of DAOs, allowing users to participate in project governance transparently and democratically. MakerDAO's DAO is an example where token holders can vote on proposed protocol changes.

Open Governance: Users' ability to directly influence protocol development and updates has introduced an open governance model, moving control from the hands of a few to the community. Continuous Technological Evolution

Interoperability: Ethereum has stimulated innovation in interoperability, enabling different blockchains to work together. Projects like Polkadot and Cosmos aim to create an interconnected ecosystem.

Transition to Ethereum 2.0: The shift to Ethereum 2.0 signifies a continued commitment to improving scalability, security, and network efficiency, which could significantly impact how DApps are developed and used.

Conclusion: Ethereum's impact on the development of decentralized applications has been monumental, marking a new era of possibilities and innovations in the blockchain world. As technology continues to evolve, the Ethereum ecosystem remains at the center of the decentralized revolution.

Chapter 7: DeFi (Decentralized Finance) on Ethereum

Key DeFi Protocols on Ethereum

Lending Protocols

Compound Finance: An automated lending and borrowing platform allowing asset deposits for secured borrowing.

Aave: A lending protocol offering the ability to deposit assets into a liquidity pool and borrow against these deposits using other assets as collateral.

Decentralized Exchanges (DEX)

Uniswap: An Automated Market Maker (AMM) protocol enabling token swaps without traditional buy or sell orders.

SushiSwap: Derived from Uniswap, offering liquidity incentives and decentralized governance functionalities.

Stablecoins

MakerDAO: A protocol issuing the DAI stablecoin using Ethereum as collateral.

USD Coin (USDC): A stablecoin pegged to the US dollar, issued by a consortium including Circle and Coinbase.

Synthetics

Synthetix: A protocol allowing the creation of synthetic tokens representing the value of other assets such as currencies, stocks, or commodities.

Impact of DeFi on Traditional Finance

Financial Accessibility: DeFi protocols provide an alternative to traditional finance, allowing anyone with an internet connection to access financial services.

Innovation in Economic Models: Introducing new models such as liquidity provisioning and yield farming, offering users opportunities for gains based on network participation.

Challenges and Perspectives

Security: DeFi protocols face security challenges, bugs, and risks inherent in their decentralized nature despite their growing popularity.

Evolution and Regulation: The rapid growth of DeFi raises regulatory and compliance questions that could influence its future growth and structure.

Conclusion

DeFi on Ethereum has revolutionized finance by making financial services accessible to everyone. As DeFi continues to evolve, its challenges and opportunities shape the financial landscape of tomorrow.

2: Analysis of Opportunities and Challenges in the DeFi Sector

Opportunities in DeFi

Financial Accessibility: DeFi eliminates traditional barriers by providing financial services to anyone with an internet connection, thus enabling financial inclusion for the unbanked.

High Potential Returns: DeFi protocols offer attractive returns through mechanisms such as yield farming, attracting numerous investors.

Innovation in Economic Models: It encourages the emergence of new economic models and decentralized governance mechanisms.

Challenges in DeFi

Security and Risks: The decentralized nature exposes DeFi protocols to security risks like smart contract code bugs and vulnerabilities.

Scalability and Costs: High transaction fees and network congestion on Ethereum limit scalability and increase costs for users.

Regulation and Compliance: Operating in a lightly regulated framework raises questions of regulation and compliance for DeFi.

Future Evolution and Perspectives

Enhanced Security: DeFi protocols are focusing on code audits, adopting improved security practices, and exploring solutions to minimize risks.

Scalability and Interoperability: Layer-two solutions and interoperability with other blockchains aim to reduce Ethereum network congestion.

Education and Adoption: Increased user awareness, better education, and an improved user experience could contribute to wider DeFi adoption.

Conclusion

While the DeFi sector presents innovative opportunities, it faces significant challenges in terms of security, regulation, and scalability. Its future evolution depends on its ability to address these challenges and leverage opportunities to create a more robust and inclusive financial ecosystem.

Chapter 8: Regulatory and Legal Evolution of Ethereum

1. Current State of Regulations Related to Ethereum Worldwide

Variable Regulatory Approaches

United States: Regulations on cryptocurrencies and tokens vary across agencies. The Securities and Exchange Commission (SEC) considers some tokens as securities, while the Commodity Futures Trading Commission (CFTC) categorizes them as commodities.

Europe: The European Union is pursuing a more nuanced approach, working on clearer and harmonized regulations for crypto-assets through the Markets in Crypto-Assets (MiCA) regulation.

Asia: Asian regulations also vary. Japan legalized cryptocurrencies as a means of payment, while China imposed severe restrictions, prohibiting certain cryptocurrency-related activities.

Current Regulatory Challenges

Classification: Token classification, especially those issued through Initial Coin Offerings (ICOs), remains unclear in many jurisdictions, leading to uncertainties about their legal status.

Legal Clarity: Lack of clear regulatory frameworks might deter businesses from fully engaging in blockchain and crypto projects, hindering innovation.

Anticipated Evolution

Regulatory Adaptation: Governments and regulators are striving to better understand and regulate the crypto space to protect investors while fostering innovation.

International Convergence: There's a trend towards international regulatory convergence to harmonize standards and facilitate cross-border exchanges within the crypto ecosystem.

Impact on Ethereum Adoption

Legal Certainty: Clear and well-defined regulations can bolster confidence among businesses and investors in Ethereum, encouraging its adoption in traditional sectors.

Compliance Challenges: Companies operating on Ethereum must adapt to changing regulations, potentially incurring additional costs and compliance challenges.

Conclusion

The global regulatory evolution significantly impacts the adoption and development of Ethereum. As regulations become more precise, it's crucial for Ethereum to navigate these changing waters to ensure its long-term legitimacy and relevance.

2 Implications of Regulatory Developments on Ethereum Adoption

Confidence and Legitimacy

Positive Impact: Clear and favorable regulations can enhance confidence among businesses and investors in Ethereum, providing it with institutional legitimacy.

Increased Adoption: Well-defined regulation can stimulate Ethereum adoption by traditional businesses seeking a stable legal framework for engaging in blockchain applications.

Reduction of Uncertainty

Investment Catalyst: Clear regulations can encourage institutional investments by removing some of the legal uncertainties associated with crypto-assets, facilitating capital inflow into the Ethereum ecosystem.

Expanded Use Cases: Clear regulation can pave the way for new use cases for Ethereum in sectors such as finance, supply chain, and governance, fostering partnerships with traditional enterprises.

Compliance and Adaptation Challenges

Compliance Costs: Regulatory requirements may add costs and operational complexity for businesses building solutions on Ethereum, especially for startups and small enterprises.

Need for Adaptation: Participants in the Ethereum ecosystem must remain agile to adapt to regulatory changes, requiring regular adjustments in processes and practices.

Innovation and Collaboration

Emergence of Standards: Regulations can incentivize the creation of standards and best practices in the Ethereum ecosystem, promoting safer and more stable environments for users and investors.

Collaboration with Regulators: Cooperation between industry players and regulators can lead to more tailored regulations and a better mutual understanding of challenges and opportunities associated with Ethereum.

Conclusion

Regulatory developments have a significant impact on Ethereum adoption. While clear regulation can foster trust and adoption, it also presents compliance and adaptation challenges for ecosystem participants. Striking a balance between innovation, compliance, and collaboration with regulators remains essential for Ethereum's future evolution in a dynamically regulated environment.

Chapter 9: The Ethereum Community

Role of the Community in Ethereum's Ongoing Development

Innovation and Contributions

Technical Development: The Ethereum community, consisting of developers, researchers, and contributors, plays a crucial role in the protocol's evolution. Ethereum Improvement Proposals (EIPs) and developments often stem from community contributions.

Education and Awareness: Community members actively engage in education and awareness efforts, spreading knowledge about Ethereum through forums, meetups, blogs, and social media.

Governance and Participation

Decentralized Governance: Ethereum's governance heavily relies on community participation. ETH holders participate in votes and proposals to shape the network's direction and updates.

Forums and Debates: Online forums like Reddit, Discord, and dedicated platforms enable the community to debate and discuss technical matters, future improvements, and challenges Ethereum faces.

Support and Diverse Ecosystem

Support and Assistance: The community offers valuable support to newcomers, providing help and resources for programming, smart contract development, and understanding Ethereum's fundamental principles.

Diversity of Contributions: The Ethereum community is diverse, with contributors from various industries, offering diverse perspectives and specific use cases for the blockchain's ongoing expansion.

Social and Cultural Impact

Cultural Creation: The community contributes to shaping a culture around Ethereum, sharing values such as decentralization, transparency, and open innovation.

Social Engagement: Community initiatives aim to use Ethereum for socially beneficial use cases, including decentralized governance, crowdfunding, and environmental impact.

Conclusion

The Ethereum community is the fundamental pillar supporting the development, adoption, and evolution of the blockchain. Its commitment, diverse contributions, and spirit of innovation contribute to shaping a dynamic and ever-evolving ecosystem.

Chapter 10: Ethereum and Technological Innovation

1 Latest Technological Developments on Ethereum

One of the most anticipated developments is the transition to Ethereum 2.0, also known as Serenity. This evolution marks a major shift from Proof-of-Work (PoW) to Proof-of-Stake (PoS), offering increased scalability, reduced energy consumption, and enhanced network security.

Significant advancements of Ethereum 2.0 include:

Beacon Chain: The launch of the Beacon Chain introduced PoS to Ethereum, laying the groundwork for Ethereum 2.0's scalability and security enhancements.

Sharding: This concept divides the Ethereum blockchain into smaller segments (shards), enabling parallel transaction processing, thereby improving the network's processing capacity.

Rollups and Optimistic Rollups: These secondary scaling solutions allow a significant number of transactions off the main chain, alleviating congestion and transaction fees.

Improvements in Layer 1 and Layer 2 In addition to Ethereum 2.0, enhancements are being made to the network's Layer 1 and Layer 2:

EIPs (Ethereum Improvement Proposals): These proposals aim to enhance Ethereum's foundation, introducing new features, performance improvements, and protocol updates.

Expansion of Layer 2 Solutions: Solutions like rollups, sidechains, and state channels continue to evolve to provide alternatives to mainnet congestion.

Advancements in Privacy and Security Efforts are also focused on enhancing privacy and security on Ethereum:

ZK-Rollups and ZK-Snarks: Zero-knowledge proofs are increasingly used to ensure transaction privacy without compromising security.

Security Enhancements: Security audits, vulnerability detection protocols, and constant updates aim to strengthen Ethereum's resilience against potential threats.

These advancements showcase the Ethereum community's ongoing commitment to improving the platform, addressing technological challenges, and creating a more robust, scalable, and secure blockchain ecosystem. These developments are crucial to supporting Ethereum's growth and widespread adoption in the years ahead.

2. Potential Impacts on the Future of Blockchain and Decentralized Applications (DApps)

Scalability and Widespread Adoption

Developments focused on Ethereum's scalability, particularly with Ethereum 2.0 and secondary scaling solutions, could address issues of congestion and high transaction costs. This could pave the way for more extensive adoption of DApps and a variety of use cases.

Diversification of Use Cases

Accumulated capacity and performance improvements in Ethereum could diversify the use cases of DApps beyond financial applications. We might witness applications in identity management, healthcare, logistics, and even governance.

Reduction of Entry Barriers for Developers

Technological improvements in Ethereum make DApp development more accessible to developers, attracting new talents and fostering innovation. This could lead to an exponential increase in the number and variety of applications built on Ethereum.

Decentralization and New Economic Models

A more evolved and secure Ethereum could contribute to strengthening the decentralization of the web, creating new economic models based on user trust and autonomy.

Institutional Adoption

If Ethereum manages to address its scalability issues while maintaining robust security, it could pave the way for broader institutional adoption. Companies might turn to Ethereum for specific use cases or to create custom blockchain solutions.

In summary, advanced Ethereum technologies are not limited to its own ecosystem; they have the potential to reshape the entire blockchain landscape and drive the global adoption of decentralized applications. These developments represent a crucial step toward realizing the vision of a more open, transparent, and equitable internet through blockchain.

Chapter 11: Economic Analysis and Price Evolution

Exploring Ethereum's economic impact and analyzing the factors influencing ETH's price.

Ethereum's Economic Ecosystem

Ethereum's internal economy is fueled by various players: miners, DApp developers, end-users, and investors. Analyzing how these parties interact, how incentives are distributed, and how transaction fees work provides insight into Ethereum's internal economy.

Transaction Pricing Models

Transaction fees on Ethereum fluctuate based on network demand. Factors such as network congestion, gas fees, and scalability improvements influence this variation. Understanding these pricing mechanisms is crucial for anticipating the network's future usage.

Analysis of Factors Influencing ETH Price

Adoption and Usage

The growing adoption of decentralized applications and DeFi protocols on Ethereum directly impacts the demand for ETH. Increased DApp usage often drives demand for ETH for transaction fees and interactions with these applications.

Technological Evolution and Updates

Technological advancements like the transition to Ethereum 2.0 can influence ETH's price by altering investors' perceptions of the network's future ability to handle demand and address scalability issues.

Market Sentiment and External Factors

ETH's price is also influenced by market sentiment, news regarding blockchain and cryptocurrencies in general, regulatory policies, and global economic events.

Perspectives on Ethereum's Economic Evolution

Analyzing Ethereum's economy and the factors influencing ETH's price provides a better understanding of the financial dynamics behind the platform. This understanding is essential for investors, developers, and anyone looking to engage with the Ethereum ecosystem.

Chapter 12: Ethical and Social Questions

Reflecting on the ethical implications of using Ethereum and its social impact.

Reflection on Ethical Implications

Decentralization and Democratization

Ethereum aims to create a decentralized ecosystem, raising questions about power distribution and governance. Who holds control? How can true democratization of the platform be ensured while avoiding concentrations of power?

Privacy and Transparency

Blockchain offers unprecedented transparency, yet it might compromise user privacy. How does Ethereum balance these aspects to ensure both transparency and data privacy?

Social Impact of Ethereum

Financial Inclusion and Accessibility

Ethereum opens doors to financial inclusion for the unbanked populations. However, technology access remains a challenge for many communities. How can Ethereum contribute to reducing these disparities?

Environmental Sustainability

Ethereum's use of Proof of Work (PoW), while transitioning to Proof of Stake (PoS), has environmental implications. How can Ethereum achieve environmental goals while continuing to innovate?

Ethics in Decentralized Applications (DApps)

Developer Responsibility

DApps built on Ethereum serve various purposes. How do developers ensure the ethical responsibility of their applications, considering potential social consequences?

Governance and Decision-Making

Governance of DApps and protocols on Ethereum raises questions about collective decision-making. How can democratic and ethical governance be ensured within these decentralized applications?

Chapter 13: Trends and Future Predictions

Exploring future forecasts and trends for Ethereum, including potential scenarios.

Understanding emerging trends and considering future scenarios for Ethereum is crucial to grasp the potential evolution of this major blockchain platform. This chapter explores forecasts and possible trends for Ethereum.

Emerging Trends

Expansion of Use Cases
Ethereum is expected to diversify its use cases beyond decentralized finance (DeFi). Areas like healthcare, governance, logistics, and intellectual property could become expansion areas for DApps on Ethereum.

Increasing Institutional Adoption
Institutional adoption of Ethereum could accelerate as the technology progresses towards better scalability with Ethereum 2.0. Companies might show more interest in customized blockchain solutions based on Ethereum.

Evolution of Governance
Governance models within the Ethereum ecosystem might evolve towards more complex and decentralized structures to better meet community needs and ensure fairer decision-making.

Possible Scenarios

Ecosystem Consolidation
A plausible scenario would be the consolidation of the Ethereum ecosystem, with tighter integration of different applications and protocols, fostering increased interoperability and synergy among projects.

Competition and Cooperation with Other Blockchains
Competition among different blockchains might intensify, but partnerships and collaborations could also multiply, enhancing interoperability between blockchain ecosystems.

Transition to Mass Adoption
If Ethereum overcomes its technical and regulatory challenges, broader adoption by the general public could become a reality. User-friendly applications and tangible use cases could lead to massive adoption.

Perspectives and Predictions

The future of Ethereum is brimming with potential and challenges. Perspectives include ongoing growth, technological innovations, and a revolution in how transactions and interactions occur online.

In summary, future trends for Ethereum point towards diversified use cases, increasing institutional adoption, and evolving governance models. Possible scenarios encompass ecosystem consolidation, closer interactions with other blockchains, and eventual mass adoption by the general public. These perspectives paint a dynamic future for Ethereum within the global blockchain ecosystem.

Chapter 14: Security and Vulnerabilities in Ethereum

1. In-Depth Analysis of Past Security Flaws on Ethereum

Security stands as a critical aspect for any blockchain platform, and Ethereum is no exception. This chapter delves into an in-depth analysis of past security flaws on Ethereum and the lessons learned from these vulnerabilities.

Analysis of Past Security Flaws on Ethereum

Smart Contract Attacks

Some of Ethereum's most infamous security flaws have been related to smart contracts. For instance, the notable incident of the DAO contract in 2016 resulted in a community split and required developer intervention.

Protocol and Update Vulnerabilities

Vulnerabilities have also been discovered in Ethereum's underlying protocols. Poorly implemented updates or bugs in the code have occasionally opened security loopholes.

User and Application Attacks

Users and applications built on Ethereum can also be targets for attacks. Scams, wallet hacks, and phishing attacks have been reported.

Lessons Learned and Current Security Measures

Development Process Improvements

Ethereum developers have strengthened their development practices, conducting more rigorous security audits and implementing stricter processes for updates.

Enhanced Protocols and Security Standards

Initiatives such as best practice development guides, security frameworks, and coding standards have been established to fortify the security of smart contracts and applications.

Awareness and Education

Security awareness has become a priority. Awareness campaigns and educational resources have been created to inform users about security best practices.

Perspectives on Ethereum Security

Past security flaws have been learning moments for Ethereum. While significant improvements have been made, security remains a constant challenge, requiring continuous vigilance and adaptation to new threats.

In summary, the analysis of past security flaws on Ethereum has led to improved development practices, strengthened protocols, and increased awareness of security. These ongoing efforts aim to bolster Ethereum's security and prevent future vulnerabilities, thereby ensuring user and developer confidence in the blockchain ecosystem.

2 Security Measures and Trends on Ethereum

Current Security Measures

Protocol Enhancements

Ethereum has undergone significant upgrades to bolster security. Changes within Ethereum 2.0, such as the transition to Proof-of-Stake (PoS), aim to enhance the network's security and energy efficiency.

Security Audits and Verifications

Security audits have become a standard for Ethereum projects. Development teams engage specialized third-party auditors to identify and resolve potential vulnerabilities before deploying smart contracts and updates.

Standards and Best Practices

Establishing security standards and development best practices is crucial. Organizations like the Ethereum Foundation and community development groups have created guides and recommendations to fortify Ethereum project security.

Security Trends on the Platform

Evolution of Threats
Attacks are constantly evolving. More sophisticated forms of attacks, such as smart contract exploits, reentrancy attacks, or front-running attacks, are emerging, requiring constant monitoring and protection.

Emerging Security Technologies
Adoption of technologies like Zero-Knowledge Proofs and advanced privacy solutions contributes to enhancing transaction security and protecting user privacy on the blockchain.

Focus on Education and Awareness
The Ethereum community emphasizes ongoing security education. Initiatives aimed at educating developers, users, and stakeholders on security practices remain at the forefront.

Future Perspectives on Security

Security on Ethereum continually evolves to address growing challenges. Technological advancements, reinforced standards, and better community collaboration contribute to preparing Ethereum to tackle future security challenges.

In summary, current security measures on Ethereum involve protocol enhancements, regular audits, the establishment of standards, and a focus on emerging threats. Security trends highlight a constant adaptation to face new threats, emphasizing the adoption of emerging technologies and ongoing education to bolster Ethereum platform security.

Chapter 15: Advanced Technical Evolution

1. Exploration of Ongoing Research and Advanced Technical Developments on Ethereum

Exploration of Ongoing Research on Ethereum

Ethereum 2.0 and PoS Implementation

Ongoing research is focused on completing Ethereum 2.0, marking the transition to Proof-of-Stake (PoS). Aspects such as finality, security, and the efficiency of the PoS consensus mechanism are under thorough study.

Sharding and Scalability

Sharding lies at the core of research to enhance Ethereum's scalability. Studies focus on methods to effectively distribute network load and enable parallel transaction processing.

Enhancements in Privacy

Research explores solutions to bolster privacy on Ethereum. Advancements in Zero-Knowledge Proofs, transaction mixing techniques, and privacy layers are being explored to enhance data protection.

Advanced Technical Developments

Rollups and Optimistic Rollups
Rollups are promising secondary scaling solutions. Research is aimed at optimizing these mechanisms to allow faster and less costly transactions on the Ethereum blockchain.

Evolutions in Smart Contracts
Research aims to enhance smart contracts by introducing more advanced standards, complex programming features, and increased interoperability with other platforms.

Focus on Interoperability and Adaptability
Work is underway to make Ethereum more compatible with other blockchains, thereby enabling smoother exchanges and interoperability among different ecosystems.

Future Perspectives on Developments

Ongoing research and advanced technical developments provide a promising outlook for Ethereum's future. The emphasis on scalability, privacy, and interoperability suggests a potential for continuous innovation within the Ethereum ecosystem.

In summary, ongoing research and advanced technical developments on Ethereum focus on Ethereum 2.0, sharding, privacy enhancement, rollups, smart contract evolution, and interoperability. These advancements pave the way for a more evolved Ethereum capable of addressing technological challenges while stimulating innovation in the blockchain universe.

2. Perspectives on Possible Protocol and Technology Evolutions Associated with Ethereum

Evolution of Consensus Protocols

Future perspectives involve continuous improvements in consensus protocols. The transition from Proof-of-Work (PoW) to Proof-of-Stake (PoS) with Ethereum 2.0 could mark the beginning of new innovations aiming to enhance security, efficiency, and environmental sustainability.

Scalability and Sharding

Future developments will focus on increased scalability through successful sharding implementation. Perspectives anticipate solutions that will enhance the network's capacity to handle more transactions simultaneously, addressing current bottlenecks.

Enhanced Privacy Approaches

Future technological advancements could strengthen privacy on Ethereum. Progress in privacy mechanisms like Zero-Knowledge

Proofs and transaction mixing techniques might offer more robust options to safeguard user privacy.

Interoperability with Other Blockchains

The future might see Ethereum develop standards and protocols for enhanced interoperability with other blockchains. This would facilitate data and value exchange between different platforms, stimulating the entire blockchain ecosystem.

Evolution of Smart Contract Standards

Perspectives envision continuous improvements in smart contract standards on Ethereum. These advancements could include more advanced programming languages, richer functionalities, and robust standards for improved security and interoperability.

Challenges and Hurdles to Overcome

Future evolutions of Ethereum won't be without challenges. Resolving issues such as governance, security, adoption, and regulation remains crucial to ensure a smooth transition to more advanced protocols and technologies.

Conclusion

Future prospects for the evolution of protocols and associated technologies with Ethereum are promising. Advanced technologies, accumulated interoperability, and feature enhancements are at the core of anticipated developments, aiming to maintain Ethereum as a leader in innovation within the blockchain ecosystem.

Chapter 16: Ethereum Economy and Ecosystem

1. **Study of Ethereum's Internal Economy, including transaction pricing models, incentives for miners and validators, etc.**

Study of Ethereum's Internal Economy

Transaction Pricing Models

Ethereum's economy relies on a transaction pricing system based on "gas." "Gas" represents the cost for performing operations on the network. Understanding how "gas" is calculated and optimized based on demand helps grasp the dynamics of transaction costs.

Incentives for Miners and Validators

Miners in Ethereum, under the current PoW system and the future transition to PoS, are incentivized to secure the network by validating transactions. PoS validators are rewarded for locking funds as collateral to participate in consensus, contributing to network security.

Inflation and Deflation Mechanisms

Understanding Ethereum's monetary policy is crucial. Currently, Ethereum has an unlimited ETH supply, although proposals for reducing inflation are under review. The transition to PoS also aims to introduce some deflation to maintain ETH's value.

Impact of Transaction Fees on Network Use

Fluctuating transaction fees influence Ethereum's usage. They can affect the viability of DApps, transaction speed, and the overall user experience on the platform.

Supply and Demand Dynamics

Increasing Use and Adoption

The rise in DApp and DeFi protocol usage fuels demand for transactions on Ethereum, impacting transaction fees and network capacity.

Factors Influencing Demand

Events like new project launches, network upgrades, blockchain-related news, and cryptocurrency market trends influence demand for Ethereum.

Economic Consequences on the Ecosystem

Balance Between Cost and Utility

Transaction pricing and incentive distribution impact user and network participant engagement. Striking a balance between transaction cost and utility is essential for maintaining a healthy ecosystem.

Adequacy of Incentive Mechanisms

Incentives for miners and validators must be balanced to ensure network security and efficiency while ensuring sufficient profitability to maintain their commitment.

Understanding Ethereum's internal economy and its influence on user behavior, network participation, and ecosystem health is pivotal for sustaining and improving the platform's functionality and utility.

2 Analysis of Ethereum's Impact on the Global Cryptocurrency Economy

Market Capitalization and Market Influence
Ethereum stands as one of the leading cryptocurrencies in terms of market capitalization, significantly shaping the cryptocurrency market dynamics. Its price movements, updates, and adoption often have a direct impact on the global market.

Stimulus for Innovation in the Blockchain Ecosystem
Ethereum has been a major catalyst for innovation in the cryptocurrency ecosystem. Its concept of smart contracts has inspired numerous new platforms and projects, contributing to the evolution and diversification of blockchain.

Evolution of Economic Models
DApps and DeFi protocols on Ethereum have introduced new economic models. Concepts like decentralized finance, liquidity pools, and non-fungible tokens (NFTs) have expanded the utility possibilities of cryptocurrencies.

Contribution to Widespread Cryptocurrency Adoption

Ethereum played a crucial role in popularizing cryptocurrencies among the general public. Varied applications and use cases demonstrated the value and potential of blockchain for real-world uses, attracting new users into the cryptocurrency ecosystem.

Impact on Finance and Financial Markets

Decentralized Finance (DeFi) Revolution

Ethereum has been fertile ground for the exponential growth of DeFi. Protocols offering loans, decentralized exchanges (DEX), and liquidity yields have disrupted traditional financial services.

Expansion of the Tokenized Economy

Ethereum's ability to issue customized tokens led to the expansion of the tokenized economy. These tokens represent diverse assets, from digital artworks to ownership fractions, opening new horizons for asset digitization.

Future Perspectives on the Cryptocurrency Economy

Evolution of Applications and Protocols

Future developments on Ethereum could continue to shape the cryptocurrency economy. Ongoing innovation in DApps, DeFi, and associated technologies could create new economic dynamics.

Increasing Integration into Traditional Economy
The growing integration of Ethereum and cryptocurrencies into
the traditional economy is anticipated. Use cases in traditional
finance, logistics, and other sectors could lead to broader
adoption.

Ethereum's impact on the global cryptocurrency economy is
significant, ranging from market capitalization to driving
innovation, expanding DeFi, and evolving economic models. This
analysis underscores Ethereum's importance in redefining the
modern financial landscape and its role as a driver for adoption
and innovation in the cryptocurrency domain.

Chapter 17: Adoption, Usage, and Real-World Use Cases

1. **Study of Ethereum's Real Use Cases in Different Sectors**

Decentralized Finance (DeFi)

Ethereum lies at the heart of the DeFi revolution. Platforms providing loans, liquidity pools, decentralized exchange protocols (DEX), and innovative financial products have flourished on Ethereum, altering the way financial services are provided and accessed.

Supply Chain and Logistics

Initiatives leverage Ethereum to track product provenance, ensure item authenticity, and enhance traceability in supply chains. These applications offer increased transparency and minimize counterfeit risks.

Decentralized Governance

Decentralized governance systems use Ethereum, enabling token holders to contribute to decisions regarding network or project evolution.

Non-Fungible Tokens (NFTs)

NFTs, issued on Ethereum, are utilized in arts, gaming, virtual real estate, etc., for creating, buying, and selling unique digital assets.

Identity and Security

Ethereum is explored for secure digital identity, storing and verifying identity information in a decentralized manner.

Advantages and Challenges of Ethereum's Use Cases

Advantages

Transparency and Immutability: Ethereum's blockchain offers transparent and immutable records, enhancing trust.

Reduced Intermediaries: Smart contracts reduce intermediaries, decreasing costs and delays.

Challenges

Scalability: Current blockchain limitations pose challenges for massive use cases.

Transaction Fees: Fluctuations can limit access for users with limited resources.

Future Perspectives of Use Cases

Evolution of Decentralized Applications (DApps)

Ongoing innovation in DApps on Ethereum could lead to new adoption areas and usage possibilities.

Integration into Traditional Sectors

Integrating Ethereum into traditional sectors could result in broader adoption and more widespread usage.

The study of Ethereum's real-world use cases demonstrates the diversity of applications and advantages provided by the blockchain. These examples showcase Ethereum's successes and challenges as a platform for decentralized and innovative applications.

2. Evaluation of Ethereum's Adoption in Enterprises and Among End Users

Adoption in Enterprises

Integration by Enterprises:
Some companies are adopting Ethereum for various applications, including finance, supply chain management, and data management solutions. They explore the benefits of smart contracts to automate and secure processes.

Development of Proprietary Solutions:
Companies are designing specific solutions based on Ethereum to meet their needs, such as asset tracking, identity management, or simplification of transactions.

Adoption Among End Users

Usage of Decentralized Applications (DApps):
Certain end users leverage Ethereum-based DApps to access financial services, invest in tokens, participate in decentralized exchanges, or interact with NFTs.

Participation in Decentralized Finance (DeFi):
End users engage in DeFi protocols on Ethereum to benefit from loans, liquidity yields, staking, yield farming, and other decentralized financial services.

Assessment of Adoption: Advantages and Limitations

Advantages of Ethereum Adoption

Decentralization and Transparency:
Users benefit from Ethereum's decentralization and transparency, allowing intermediary-free interactions and immutable data.

Range of Applications:
Ethereum's ecosystem offers a variety of applications, from finance to governance, providing users with a broad range of possibilities.

Limitations and Challenges

Complexity of Use:
For non-technical users, interacting with Ethereum and its applications can be complex, requiring an in-depth understanding of cryptocurrencies.

Transaction Fees and Scalability:
Fluctuating transaction fees and scalability challenges may limit adoption for users seeking low-cost and fast transactions on a large scale.

Future Perspectives on Adoption

Simplification of User Experience

Efforts are underway to make interacting with Ethereum more user-friendly, reducing complexity for end users and promoting broader adoption.

Scalability and Fee Reduction

Planned technical advancements, notably with Ethereum 2.0, aim to enhance scalability and reduce transaction fees, making the platform more attractive to a larger user base.

The evaluation of Ethereum's adoption in enterprises and among end users highlights both successes and challenges. The benefits of decentralization and application diversity are evident, but limitations such as usage complexity and fluctuating costs need to be addressed for more widespread adoption.

Chapter 18: Education, Training, and Resources

1. Learning and Training Resources on Ethereum: Guides, Tutorials, and Best Practices

Guides and Tutorials

Official Ethereum Documentation: Ethereum's official guides and documentation provide a solid foundation for understanding fundamental concepts, features, and development procedures on the platform.

Online Communities and Forums: Platforms like Reddit (r/ethereum) or discussion platforms like Ethereum Stack Exchange offer interactive discussions, tutorials, and answers to specific questions from developers and users.

Courses and Learning Programs

Online Courses: Educational platforms like Coursera, Udemy, and Ethereum Foundation's Ethereum.org offer dedicated Ethereum courses, ranging from basics to advanced topics for developers and users.

Workshops and Events: Workshops and events organized by developers and experts provide opportunities for hands-on learning, networking, and sharing best practices.

Development Tools

Development Environments: Tools like Truffle, Remix, and Hardhat provide development environments for writing, testing, and deploying smart contracts and decentralized applications on Ethereum.

References and Standards: Libraries like OpenZeppelin offer smart contract standards and reusable libraries, facilitating secure development on the Ethereum blockchain.

Importance of Educational Resources

Enhancing Understanding and Adoption Access to quality educational resources on Ethereum is crucial for democratizing the technology, enhancing understanding, and encouraging wider adoption.

Supporting Innovation and Development Well-supported resources foster innovation by providing developers with the tools and knowledge necessary to create new applications and improve the Ethereum ecosystem.

Challenges and Future Perspectives

Democratizing Access to Education Accessibility remains a challenge. Continuing to make educational resources available in multiple languages and financially accessible is essential to reach a more diverse audience.

Evolving with Technology Given the rapid evolution of blockchain technology, educational resources must be continually updated to reflect new developments and best practices.

Educational resources on Ethereum, ranging from guides and tutorials to online courses and development tools, play a crucial role in learning and development on the platform. These resources not only support the education of users and developers but also encourage ongoing innovation within the Ethereum ecosystem.

2. Ethereum Education and Awareness Initiatives Worldwide

University and Academic Programs

Courses and Certifications: Some universities offer specific academic programs on Ethereum, including courses on smart contracts, blockchain, and decentralized application development.

Hackathons and Competitions: Events organized in universities, such as hackathons, encourage students to explore Ethereum, develop applications, and present innovative ideas.

Communities and Non-Profit Organizations

Meetup Groups and Workshops: Local groups of enthusiasts organize meetups and workshops to share knowledge, discuss use cases, and facilitate hands-on interaction with Ethereum.

Community Projects: Volunteer initiatives educate the general public through awareness projects, documentation translated into different languages, and mentorship programs.

Contributions from Enterprises and Foundations

Corporate Training Programs: Some companies integrate Ethereum into their internal training programs to familiarize their employees with blockchain technology.
Foundation Support: Foundations like the Ethereum Foundation invest in global educational initiatives, supporting training programs, hackathons, and academic research.

Impact of Educational Initiatives

Raising Awareness and Democratizing Technology These educational initiatives contribute to raising awareness about Ethereum to a broader audience, demystifying blockchain technology, and encouraging exploration of its applications.

Encouraging Innovation and Development By providing accessible educational resources, these initiatives have led to the emergence of new ideas, the creation of innovative projects, and the development of skills in the blockchain domain.

Challenges and Future Perspectives

Continuous Need for Education Technology evolves rapidly, necessitating the maintenance of updated educational programs to reflect recent developments on Ethereum.

Accessibility and Broadening Target Audiences Expanding educational programs to reach diverse audiences, including those from underrepresented regions, requires a focus on accessibility and inclusion.

Education and awareness initiatives on Ethereum, led by universities, communities, businesses, or non-profit organizations, play a vital role in spreading knowledge about blockchain technology. These efforts contribute to building a strong foundation for broader adoption and continuous development within the Ethereum ecosystem.

Chapter 19: Summary of External Perspectives

This chapter presents insights from external experts offering varied perspectives on the future of Ethereum and blockchain technology.

Industry Leaders' Vision

Prominent Developers: Interviews with leading developers on Ethereum provide insights into technical developments and future challenges for the platform.

Economists and Analysts: Perspectives from economists and analysts offer a macroeconomic view of Ethereum's impact on financial markets and the global economy.

Experiences of Users and Enterprises

End-User Testimonials: Detailed narratives from end-users outline their positive and negative experiences with Ethereum, highlighting real-world benefits and challenges.

Enterprise Perspectives: Contributions from companies utilizing Ethereum offer insights into specific use cases, observed advantages, and necessary adaptations.

Regulatory and Institutional Views

Regulators and Legislators: Views from regulators on the evolution of regulatory frameworks related to Ethereum and blockchain provide insights into regulatory trends.

Institutional Investors: Opinions from institutional investors on the financial future of blockchain and Ethereum offer significant financial and strategic perspectives.

Diverse Perspectives for Comprehensive Understanding

Anticipated Trends and Challenges Varied perspectives indicate emerging trends and anticipated challenges for Ethereum, including analyses on scalability, regulation, and adoption.

Insights into Technological Evolution External experts share their visions regarding expected future technological developments, such as the evolution of PoS, scalability solutions, and interoperability with other blockchains.

Conclusion on External Perspectives

Contributions from external experts offer a crucial diversity of viewpoints for understanding the multiple facets of Ethereum and blockchain's future evolution. These perspectives enrich the overall vision, allowing anticipation of potential developments and forthcoming challenges.

Chapter 20: Global and Geopolitical Perspectives

This chapter delves into the analysis of Ethereum's impact and adoption across diverse geographical and socio-economic contexts worldwide.

Adoption in Different Countries

North America: Analysis of Ethereum's increasing adoption and usage in the United States and Canada, along with its impact on traditional financial markets.

Europe: Examination of Ethereum's integration in European countries, highlighting specific regulations and government initiatives, whether favorable or restrictive.

Asia-Pacific: Analysis of Ethereum's rapid adoption in Asian countries, its impact on technological and financial sectors, and regulatory trends in the region.

Inequalities and Adoption Diversity

Developing Regions: Study of initiatives using Ethereum to address socio-economic issues in developing countries, exploring barriers to adoption.

Adoption Disparities: Analysis of adoption disparities among different regions due to socio-economic, regulatory, and technological factors.

Geopolitical Impact of Ethereum

Geopolitical Consequences

Impact on Financial Systems: Evaluation of how Ethereum's adoption may disrupt traditional financial systems and influence global economic dynamics.

Geopolitics and Technological Innovation: Analysis of the geopolitical impact of the blockchain innovation race, highlighting government initiatives and rivalries between countries.

Implications for Sovereignty and Policy

Digital Sovereignty: Reflection on the implications of Ethereum's rise and decentralized technologies on national sovereignty and global governance.

Regulation and Public Policies: Analysis of government responses to Ethereum's rise, including regulatory policies and efforts to stimulate or curb adoption.

Future Perspectives of Geographical Adoption

Economic and Social Development

Potential for Inequality Reduction: Reflection on Ethereum's potential to improve financial access and reduce economic disparities in different regions.

Innovation Stimulus: Anticipation of Ethereum's catalyzing effect on innovation and economic development, especially in emerging economies.

Evolution of Geopolitical Dynamics

Emergence of Tech Hubs: Prediction about the emergence of tech hubs based on Ethereum and their effects on geopolitics and the global economy.

Role of International Cooperation: Perspectives on the need for international cooperation to effectively regulate and integrate Ethereum within the global geopolitical context.

The analysis of Ethereum's global and geopolitical perspectives aids in understanding the differentiated impact of blockchain technology in various socio-economic and geographical contexts. This evaluation emphasizes the importance of considering geopolitical aspects in the development and adoption of technologies like Ethereum.

Chapter 21: Partnerships and Collaborations

This chapter focuses on Ethereum's collaborations with other renowned blockchains and protocols.

Collaboration with Other Blockchains

Interoperability between Blockchains:

Analysis of initiatives establishing bridges between Ethereum and other major blockchains, enabling asset and data exchange between networks.

Decentralized Exchange Protocols (DEX):

Examination of inter-chain DEX protocols facilitating asset exchange across different blockchains, providing increased liquidity and interoperability.

Collaboration for Technological Innovation

Development Partnerships:

Examination of partnerships between Ethereum and other renowned protocols to collaborate on technical solutions such as scalability or privacy.

Joint Research Initiatives:

Analysis of collaborative research projects between Ethereum and other blockchains to explore new advanced technologies and address common issues.

Benefits of Partnerships for Ethereum

Expansion of Capabilities

Enhanced Scalability:

Collaborations aim to improve Ethereum's scalability by exploring solutions like sharding or rollups, leveraging external innovations.

Diversification of Use Cases:

Collaboration opens new use cases by integrating unique features from other blockchains into the Ethereum ecosystem.

Strengthening the Blockchain Ecosystem

Increased Network Effects:

Partnerships strengthen the overall blockchain ecosystem by encouraging adoption and stimulating innovation through resource and knowledge sharing.

Reducing Entry Barriers:

Collaboration can reduce adoption barriers by offering transparent and user-friendly cross-chain solutions.

Future Perspectives of Partnerships

Expansion of Alliances

New Protocols and Networks:

Anticipation of new collaborations with emerging protocols or niche blockchain networks to enrich the Ethereum ecosystem.

Increased Interconnectivity:

Forecasting accumulated interconnectivity between blockchains, creating a more interoperable and synergistic blockchain ecosystem.

Impact on Adoption and Innovation

Adoption Acceleration:

Partnerships may expedite Ethereum adoption by offering extended functionalities and broadening the spectrum of use cases.

Catalyst for Innovation:

Collaborations support continuous innovation by fostering the exchange of ideas and solutions among various blockchain entities.

Ethereum's partnerships and collaborations with other blockchains and renowned protocols represent a key strategy to enhance scalability, interoperability, and blockchain technology adoption. These alliances foster innovation and strengthen the overall blockchain ecosystem.

2 Impact of Partnerships on the Ethereum Ecosystem and Blockchain in General

Expanding Utility and Functionality

Diversification of Use Cases: Partnerships introduce new use cases and functionalities to Ethereum, broadening its appeal to a wider audience.

Improving Interoperability: Collaborations strengthen interoperability, facilitating the exchange of assets and data across different platforms, thereby increasing the value of the Ethereum ecosystem.

Technological Advancements and Innovation

Resource Sharing: Partnerships enable the sharing of resources and knowledge, accelerating the development of innovative solutions and global technological progress.

Co-creation of Solutions: Collaborations encourage the co-creation of technical solutions and the exploration of new advancements, solidifying Ethereum's position as a blockchain leader.

Impact on the Blockchain as a Whole

Effect on Adoption and Blockchain Awareness

Boosting Adoption: Partnerships enhance the credibility of the blockchain, attracting attention from users and businesses interested in this technology.

Enhancing Trust: Successful partnerships reinforce trust in the blockchain by demonstrating its viability and integration into real-world applications.

Catalyst for Sectoral Innovation

Standard Development: Collaborations contribute to establishing standards and best practices, fostering an environment conducive to continuous innovation.

Use Case Experimentation: Collaborations enable the experimentation of various use cases, stimulating innovation across diverse sectors.

Future Perspectives on Partnership Impacts

Growth of the Blockchain Ecosystem

Expansion of Collaborations: The future promises more inter-chain collaborations and strategic alliances to enrich the ecosystem.

Emergence of New Opportunities: Partnerships pave the way for new innovation and adoption opportunities, generating new use cases and experiences for users.

Impact on Technological Maturity

Consolidation of Standards: Increased partnerships lead to standard consolidation, stabilizing blockchain technology as a whole.

Growth of Confidence and Stability: Successful collaborations enhance confidence and stabilize the image of blockchain as a resilient technology.

Partnerships play a pivotal role in the expansion, adoption, and innovation of the Ethereum ecosystem and blockchain. They drive interoperability, foster innovation, and bolster the credibility of the technology, paving the way for new advancements and opportunities in the future.

Chapter 22: Advanced Concepts and Technical Developments

1. In-depth Exploration of Emerging Concepts: Rollups and Layer 2 Scaling Solutions

Rollups: A Major Evolution Rollups signify a significant innovation within the Ethereum landscape, providing a promising solution to significantly enhance the network's processing capacity. These solutions, collectively termed "rollups," propose an innovative way to manage transactions off the main blockchain, relieving congestion and improving efficiency.

The essence of Rollups lies in their ability to aggregate multiple transactions into a single one, compressing data for lighter and faster inclusion on the main chain. They come in two main types: Optimistic Rollups and ZK-Rollups (Zero-Knowledge).

Optimistic Rollups: These optimize transaction management by bundling numerous operations into a single transaction, notably reducing the load on the main blockchain. This results in significant improvements in performance and cost.

ZK-Rollups (Zero-Knowledge): These Rollups utilize advanced cryptographic techniques to prove transaction validity without needing to disclose specific transaction details. This ensures privacy while enhancing scalability.

Secondary Scaling Solutions Besides Rollups, secondary scaling solutions represent another vital dimension for Ethereum's expansion. They offer alternative methods to handle a large volume of transactions off the main chain, thereby enhancing scalability without compromising security or decentralization.

These secondary solutions can take different forms, such as sidechains or scaling networks, each with its specific advantages in terms of performance, cost, and security. Their aim is to alleviate pressure on the main blockchain while maintaining a high level of security and decentralization.

In conclusion, the emergence of Rollups and secondary scaling solutions marks a crucial step in Ethereum's evolution. These innovations promise not only to significantly enhance the network's performance but also to pave the way for new use cases and wider adoption, propelling Ethereum towards new heights in the realm of blockchain and decentralized applications.

2. Advancements in Privacy and Security: Zero-Knowledge Proofs, Privacy Techniques

Zero-Knowledge Proofs: Safeguarding Identity Advancements in privacy within the Ethereum blockchain are crucial for ensuring the protection of users' sensitive data. Zero-Knowledge Proofs (ZKPs) stand out as one of the most notable advancements in this field.

ZKPs enable proving the truth of information without revealing the details of that information. This means a person can prove they possess specific knowledge without disclosing that knowledge itself. On Ethereum, this translates to transactions and interactions where only the directly involved parties have knowledge of the details, preserving data confidentiality.

Privacy Techniques: Enhancing Security In addition to ZKPs, emerging innovative privacy techniques aim to enhance transaction and interaction security on the blockchain. These techniques focus on encrypting data in sophisticated ways, ensuring that only authorized parties can access exchanged information.

Among these techniques is homomorphic encryption, enabling calculations on encrypted data without decrypting it, thereby preserving data confidentiality while allowing processing. This advancement offers an added layer of data protection, strengthening users' trust in Ethereum network security.

In summary, advancements in privacy and security, such as Zero-Knowledge Proofs and advanced privacy techniques, contribute to bolstering user confidence by ensuring the protection of their personal data and transactions on the Ethereum blockchain. This opens the door to broader adoption and more diversified applications of this revolutionary technology.

Chapter 23: Retrospective of Ethereum Versions

1. Detailed History of Previous Ethereum Versions

Ethereum 1.0: Emergence

The initial Ethereum version, launched in 2015, marked a fundamental step in blockchain history. It introduced smart contracts and established the foundation for decentralization, empowering developers to create decentralized applications (DApps) and deploy autonomous contracts.

Major Updates and Functional Evolution

Over time, Ethereum has undergone several significant updates, each bringing notable changes:

Homestead (2016):
Consolidated the security and stability of the Ethereum network, marking a substantial step toward the platform's maturity.

Metropolis (Byzantium and Constantinople - 2017-2019):
This phase brought significant improvements in terms of privacy, security, and functionality, notably with the introduction of the concept of ZKP (Zero-Knowledge Proofs) and new opcodes.

Istanbul (2019):
Introduced performance enhancements and adjustments to the fee system to make the network more efficient.

Berlin (2021):
Aimed at optimizing network operations, this update improved transaction efficiency and strengthened security.

Towards Ethereum 2.0: The Transition

Simultaneously, Ethereum 2.0 emerged as a major overhaul of the network, aiming to address scalability and energy consumption issues inherent in Ethereum 1.0. This transition to Ethereum 2.0 involves shifting from Proof of Work (PoW) to Proof of Stake (PoS) and introducing sharding to enhance the network's transaction processing capacity.

Impact of Updates on Community and Adoption

Every Ethereum update and evolution has had a significant impact on the developer, miner, and user community. These changes have shaped the user experience, network efficiency, and often sparked discussions around scalability and platform governance.

In conclusion, this retrospective of previous Ethereum versions illustrates the impressive evolution of this platform since its inception. It demonstrates how each update has contributed to shaping the blockchain, addressing issues, and laying the groundwork for Ethereum's ever-evolving technology.

2 Impacts of Updates on the Ethereum Community and Adoption

Impacts of Updates on Community and Adoption

The various versions and updates of Ethereum have had significant implications for the community, users, and the overall adoption of the blockchain platform.

Community Engagement

Each new version has led to a high level of engagement within the Ethereum community. Developers, miners, and users often actively contribute to discussions, testing, and implementation of new features. These updates have often been the result of a decentralized decision-making process involving a wide range of stakeholders, reinforcing the collaborative nature of the platform.

Impact on Users

Updates have often enhanced the Ethereum user experience. Adjustments in transaction fees, improvements in network speed and efficiency, and the introduction of new features have made the platform more user-friendly and appealing to a broader audience.

Adoption and New Use Cases

Each update has opened new opportunities and use cases for Ethereum. Improvements in security, privacy, and processing capacity have facilitated the emergence of new decentralized applications (DApps) and strengthened Ethereum's appeal across sectors such as finance, logistics, and decentralized governance.

Concerns and Debates

However, these updates have not been without debates and concerns within the community. Major updates, such as the transition to Ethereum 2.0, have sparked discussions on governance, security, and implications for miners and ETH holders.

Evolution and Adaptation

Ultimately, each update has acted as a catalyst for Ethereum's evolution, prompting the community to adapt, innovate, and address technical challenges while maintaining commitment to the vision of decentralization and accessibility.

Conclusion : The impacts of Ethereum updates go far beyond technical modifications. They have shaped the culture, adoption, and future direction of the platform, highlighting the crucial importance of the interaction between technology and the community in advancing a blockchain platform of such magnitude.

Chapter 24: In-Depth Social Impact and Ethical Considerations

2   Deep Reflections on the Positive Social Impact and Ethical Challenges Associated with the Use of Ethereum in Different Socioeconomic Contexts.

The use of Ethereum generates significant social impact in diverse socio-economic contexts, presenting opportunities while posing ethical challenges that require careful consideration.

Financial Inclusion:

Ethereum, through decentralized applications (DApps) and DeFi, offers solutions for financial inclusion, granting access to financial services previously unavailable to many individuals in underbanked regions or within restrictive traditional financial systems.

Transparency and Governance:

The transparency of the blockchain provides opportunities for improved governance across various sectors, allowing for greater accountability and participation among stakeholders.

Reduction of Intermediaries:

By eliminating intermediaries, Ethereum can reduce costs and increase efficiency in areas such as financial transactions, insurance, and logistics.

Ethical Challenges to Consider

Data Security:

The transparency of the blockchain might present challenges regarding the privacy and security of personal data, necessitating additional measures to protect sensitive information.

Equality and Accessibility:

Despite its potential benefits, Ethereum could exacerbate digital inequalities if access to the technology and the necessary education to benefit from it is not evenly distributed.

Responsibility and Regulation:

Decentralization might complicate accountability in cases of abusive behaviors or illicit transactions, requiring thoughtful consideration of regulation without disrupting the fundamental values of the blockchain.

Importance of Ethical Evaluation

Conducting rigorous ethical evaluations and continuing Ethereum's use across various contexts is crucial. Balancing technological innovation with social and ethical implications must be constantly reassessed to ensure that socio-economic benefits are not achieved at the expense of ethics and fundamental human values.

In conclusion, this comprehensive examination of the social impact and ethical challenges associated with using Ethereum underscores the crucial importance of considering social, ethical, and moral implications in the deployment and evolution of this technology to promote a sustainable, fair, and inclusive future.

2 Potential of Ethereum for Empowerment and Inequality Reduction

Empowerment Through Decentralization

Ethereum holds remarkable potential to empower individuals and communities while contributing to reducing existing inequalities in certain regions or industries.

Access to Financial Services:

In underbanked or underserved regions by traditional financial institutions, Ethereum offers direct access to financial services through DApps and DeFi, enabling individuals to have control over their finances.

Opportunities for Small Businesses:

The Ethereum blockchain provides opportunities for small businesses by streamlining business processes and particularly transaction costs, opening new markets, and enhancing competitiveness.

Transparency and Autonomy:

The transparency and immutability of the blockchain allow individuals to have more direct control over their data and assets, thereby strengthening their autonomy and security.

Inequality Reduction Through Innovation

Ethereum, with its decentralized architecture and advanced functionalities, has the potential to reduce disparities across various sectors.

Education and Access to Information:

By facilitating access to education and information through decentralized platforms, Ethereum can help bridge knowledge gaps in regions with limited access to information.

Emerging Economies:

In emerging economies, Ethereum can serve as a catalyst to drive innovation, create job opportunities, and foster economic development.

Decentralized Governance:

Decentralized governance allows marginalized communities to have a more active role in decision-making, addressing power asymmetries in certain contexts.

Aspirations for a Fair Future

While Ethereum's potential for empowerment and inequality reduction is significant, its full realization depends on equity in access to technology, education, and resources necessary for full participation in this ecosystem.

In conclusion, this examination of Ethereum's potential for empowerment and inequality reduction highlights the substantial opportunities offered by this technology. However, achieving these goals requires continued commitment to equity and inclusion, along with concerted efforts to overcome barriers to adoption and participation, creating a more equitable and inclusive future.

Chapter 25: International Adoption and Geopolitics

1. **Deep analysis of Ethereum adoption in various countries and regions, highlighting obstacles, opportunities, and cultural differences.**

The adoption of Ethereum varies significantly from one country to another and is influenced by a myriad of factors, including economic conditions, regulations, and cultural differences. This comprehensive analysis delves into these differences to better understand the obstacles, opportunities, and diverse geopolitical dynamics associated with Ethereum adoption.

Obstacles and Challenges

Regulation and Legislation:
Divergent regulations in different countries can create challenges for widespread Ethereum adoption. Some governments have adopted restrictive approaches to cryptocurrencies, posing regulatory barriers.

Infrastructure and Access:
Disparities in technological infrastructure and internet access in certain regions can limit Ethereum adoption, making blockchain use difficult or impossible for some populations.

Trust and Education:
Limited understanding of blockchain technology and distrust in new technologies can be barriers to adoption.

Opportunities and Potential

Emergence of New Markets:
In some developing countries, Ethereum paves the way for new economic markets, offering opportunities for innovation and growth.

Role in Innovation:
Ethereum adoption in progressive regions is often associated with innovative initiatives in sectors like finance, healthcare, and governance.

Cultural Diversity:
Cultural diversity impacts how Ethereum is perceived and adopted, with some countries placing more value on decentralization and transparency than others.

Cultural and Geopolitical Differences

Cultural differences play a major role in Ethereum adoption, shaping attitudes and behaviors toward the technology.

Government Approaches:
Governments' attitudes toward cryptocurrencies and blockchain technology vary, influencing the regulatory environment and Ethereum adoption.

User Behavior:
Cultures that value trust and transparency might be more inclined to adopt Ethereum for its decentralized aspects.

Education and Awareness:
How education and awareness are conducted can influence the understanding and acceptance of Ethereum in different cultures.

Geopolitical Conclusion

In conclusion, the analysis of Ethereum's international adoption highlights the challenges, opportunities, and cultural nuances shaping its adoption worldwide. Understanding these geopolitical dynamics is crucial to foster broader and more inclusive Ethereum adoption while enabling the technology to significantly contribute to global innovation, economic growth, and social transformation.

2. **The increasing adoption of the Ethereum blockchain holds profound geopolitical implications, redefining global economic, political, and social dynamics.**

Transformation of Economic Exchanges

New Trade Relationships:
Ethereum's emergence has the potential to reshape international trade relationships by enabling direct and transparent exchanges between entities, often bypassing traditional economic structures.

Challenges and Opportunities for States:
States are faced with the need to adapt their economic and fiscal policies to integrate the blockchain economy. This creates opportunities for some and challenges for others, affecting national competitive advantages.

Redefining Governance Models

Decentralization and Power:
Ethereum adoption challenges centralized governance models by offering decentralized alternatives. This redistributes economic and political power, impacting traditional governance structures.

Digital Diplomacy:
Digital diplomacy emerges as a new area where the promotion of
blockchain technology, including Ethereum, can become a
strategic issue in international relations.

Security and Geopolitics

Cybersecurity and Sovereignty:
Ethereum adoption raises concerns about data security and
sovereignty, requiring international cooperation to ensure the
protection of national interests.

New Forms of Cooperation:
The Ethereum blockchain can encourage new forms of
cooperation between nations, particularly in combating fraud,
corruption, and money laundering.

Social and Cultural Repercussions

Cultural Transformation:
Ethereum adoption impacts culture, fostering values of trust,
transparency, and individual autonomy often encouraged by
blockchain technology.

Education and Workforce:
Nations investing in education and training on blockchain,
including Ethereum, can develop a skilled workforce for the
future.

Geopolitical Conclusion

In summary, the growing adoption of the Ethereum blockchain resonates beyond national borders, reshaping global economic, political, and cultural relations. How states, organizations, and individuals adapt to this geopolitical transformation will largely determine the direction and magnitude of Ethereum blockchain's impact on the international stage.

Chapter 26: Addressing Advanced Questions

1. **Thorough Exploration of Ethereum's Complex Governance, Scalability, and Other Technical Challenges.**

Decentralized Governance:

The decentralized governance of Ethereum raises intricate questions. How can evolutionary decisions be made without excessive centralization? What mechanisms ensure fair representation of involved parties? Detailed exploration of these questions aims to define robust and participatory governance models.

Scalability and Evolution:

Challenges regarding Ethereum's scalability are critical. How can fast processing times and low transaction fees be maintained as the network grows? Exploring scaling solutions like sharding and potential trade-offs is essential for ensuring the network's sustainability.

Interoperability with Other Blockchains:

Compatibility and interoperability among different blockchains pose complex issues. How can seamless communication between Ethereum and other networks be ensured without compromising security? In-depth exploration of interoperability protocols like blockchain bridges is necessary for facilitating wider adoption.

Environmental Sustainability:

The transition from Proof of Work (PoW) to Proof of Stake (PoS) aims to improve Ethereum's environmental sustainability. How can energy impact be minimized while maintaining security and decentralization? A thorough analysis of PoS implications on network security and ecological footprint is crucial.

Challenges and Solutions: Holistic Approach

Navigating Governance Complexity:

Implementing decentralized governance mechanisms like DAOs can enable transparent and inclusive decision-making. However, this requires ongoing education of stakeholders and continuous adaptation to the network's evolving realities.

Strategies for Scalability:

Integrating scaling solutions such as sharding and rollups aims to increase network capacity. Nevertheless, close monitoring of the efficiency of these solutions and adaptation to emerging challenges as blockchain technology evolves are crucial.

Secure Interoperability:

Developing interoperable standards and secure protocols facilitates the exchange of information and assets between different blockchains. Adoption of standards like ERC-20 and ERC-721 demonstrates the path to smoother interoperability.

Environmental Transition:

The move to PoS is a step toward environmental sustainability. However, it requires careful management of economic incentives and regular monitoring of network performance to ensure optimal security while reducing the carbon footprint.

Conclusion: Ethereum's Constant Evolution

In conclusion, addressing Ethereum's advanced questions requires a holistic approach, combining technical innovation, participatory governance models, and constant adaptation to the changing needs of the community. Detailed exploration of these challenges ensures the continuous and sustainable evolution of the Ethereum blockchain.

2. Solutions for Advanced Challenges

Enhanced DAOs: Developing more sophisticated DAOs with improved voting mechanisms and better token holder representation.

Scalability Solutions:

Sharding Implementation: Gradual deployment of sharding to enhance Ethereum's network capacity in handling larger transaction volumes.

Optimization of Rollups: Continuous refinement of rollup solutions for maximal efficiency in transaction processing.

Interoperability with Other Blockchains:

Interoperability Standards: Establishing interoperable standards to facilitate the exchange of assets and information between different blockchains.

Improved Bridge Protocols: Developing more secure blockchain bridge protocols for smoother interoperability.

Environmental Sustainability Solutions:

Proof of Stake Optimization: Continual optimization of proof of stake to minimize the carbon footprint while ensuring network security.

Responsible Transition: A gradual and cautious transition from proof of work to proof of stake to mitigate impacts on security and the environment.

Approach and Future Perspectives

Collaboration and Innovation:

Ongoing Collaboration: Encouraging collaboration among developers, researchers, and the community to explore and implement these solutions.

Continuous Innovation: Fostering a culture of continual innovation to adapt to new challenges and opportunities emerging in the Ethereum ecosystem.

Chapter 27: Current Developments and Projects to Watch

1. **Highlighting Projects Currently in Development, Upcoming Updates, and Emerging Trends in the Ethereum Ecosystem.**

Ongoing Development Projects

Rollup Optimization:

Numerous teams are working on enhancing rollups, secondary scaling solutions aimed at increasing the efficiency and speed of transactions on the Ethereum blockchain.

Bridge Protocol Development:

Projects are focusing on strengthening bridge protocols between different blockchains to improve interoperability and facilitate the exchange of assets across networks.

DAO Improvement:

Considerable efforts are directed toward enhancing DAOs, with a particular focus on governance and token holder representation for more equitable participation.

Upcoming Updates

Transition to Ethereum 2.0:

The upcoming phases of Ethereum 2.0, especially the ongoing deployment of PoS and the gradual introduction of sharding, are highly anticipated to enhance scalability and environmental sustainability.

Protocol Evolutions:

Significant protocol updates are planned to improve the security, efficiency, and interoperability of Ethereum, thereby creating opportunities for new applications and use cases.

Emerging Trends

Decentralized Finance (DeFi):

The DeFi sector on Ethereum continues to grow, with new protocols and applications expanding possibilities for decentralized lending, trading, and staking.

New Use Cases:

Emerging trends showcase Ethereum exploration in areas such as digital art (NFTs), decentralized governance, and the tokenization of real-world assets.

Security Research:

Particular attention is being paid to security research, with initiatives aimed at identifying and addressing potential vulnerabilities on the Ethereum blockchain.

Future Perspectives

Current developments and ongoing projects bring a dynamic and ever-evolving Ethereum ecosystem. By closely monitoring these advancements, it's possible to anticipate future trends and identify emerging opportunities that will shape the future of the Ethereum blockchain and its decentralized applications.

2. Potential Impact of These Developments on Ethereum and Blockchain's Future

Technological Evolution

Scalability and Adoption:

Improvements in scalability like sharding and widespread rollup implementation could reduce transaction fees and accelerate processing times, fostering wider adoption of Ethereum across various sectors.

Security and Trust:

Advancements in security bolster user and corporate trust in Ethereum's reliability, stimulating new use cases and attracting more institutional investors.

Impact on the Financial Ecosystem

DeFi Consolidation:

A more mature and secure DeFi attracts larger financial flows, creating new investment opportunities and broadening Ethereum's role in the global financial system.

Tokenization of Real Assets:

Expanding the tokenization of real assets, such as real estate or artworks, opens new markets and offers greater accessibility to traditionally less liquid assets.

Influence on Innovation

Adoption by Other Industries:

Ethereum's evolution toward more scalable and secure solutions attracts attention from industries beyond finance, fostering innovation and integrating blockchain technology into diverse sectors.

Emergence of New Economic Models:

Technological improvements enable the emergence of new economic and decentralized governance models, reshaping how businesses and communities interact and operate.

Anticipating Challenges

Complexity of Updates:

Major updates might face compatibility and transition challenges, requiring transparent communication and gradual adoption to minimize disruptions.

Maintaining Decentralization:

Growth and increasing complexity could challenge the maintenance of decentralization and democratic principles at Ethereum's core.

Conclusion: Evolution and Adaptation

Current and future developments in Ethereum promise a significant evolution in blockchain technology, paving the way for new possibilities and challenges. The impact of these advancements will depend on how the Ethereum community manages transitions, anticipates challenges, and seizes opportunities to shape a sustainable and innovative future for the Ethereum blockchain.

Conclusion: Recapitulation of Key Points

Our journey through the Ethereum universe has unveiled a revolutionary blockchain platform with immense potential and unique challenges. Here's a summary of the key takeaways:

Blockchain Revolution

Ethereum, Pillar of Innovation:
Introducing smart contracts and a programmable platform, Ethereum paved the way for a multitude of decentralized use cases.

Evolution and Advancements:
Ethereum's evolution, from PoW to PoS, from sharding to rollups, signifies a constant pursuit of scalability, security, and sustainability.

Impact on Economy and Society

DeFi and New Financial Models:
Decentralized finance has reshaped traditional financial models, presenting new opportunities and challenges.

Reflection on Social Impact:
Ethereum's use prompts reflections on empowerment, inequality reduction, and ethical implications across varied socio-economic contexts.

Geopolitical Dynamics

Global Adoption: Ethereum's adoption varies across regions due to different regulations, infrastructures, and cultural perceptions.

Geopolitical Impact: The increasing adoption of Ethereum's blockchain redefines global economic, political, and cultural relationships.

Future Challenges and Opportunities

Solutions for the Future: Challenges like governance, scalability, and security find solutions in continuous innovation and community collaboration.

Outlook for Ethereum: Current and upcoming developments will shape Ethereum's future by impacting the economy, society, and international relations.

In essence, Ethereum isn't just a technology; it's a transformative force. Its future relies on the community's ability to tackle challenges while leveraging opportunities, shaping a landscape where decentralization, innovation, and individual autonomy converge toward a promising horizon.

The discovery of the Ethereum universe has immersed us in the heart of an unprecedented technological and social revolution. This journey, rich in discoveries, has explored the foundations, advancements, and implications of a revolutionary blockchain.

Ethereum has paved the way for an era where trust and transparency no longer depend on intermediaries but rely on autonomous and decentralized protocols. Its introduction of smart contracts has opened a horizon of endless possibilities, transforming sectors such as finance, governance, and artistic creativity.

This constant evolution, from its early days to the transition towards Ethereum 2.0, reflects a determination to address technical challenges while meeting the changing needs of a global community.

Yet, with innovation and opportunities, also come profound reflections. The social, economic, and geopolitical impact of Ethereum manifests through debates on governance, equality, and redefined international relations.

The future of Ethereum lies in the ability to merge innovation and ethics, to maintain decentralization while managing the increasing complexity of technology. It's an exciting challenge where each development, each project, shapes a more resilient and inclusive ecosystem.

Thus, referencing this book, we contemplate a horizon where the Ethereum blockchain, more than just technology, embodies a vision for a fairer, transparent, and interconnected world. A future where decentralization transcends borders to give rise to new forms of trust, collaboration, and endless possibilities.